TOTALLY WEIRD
Plants

Contents

Tricky words are explained on page 32.

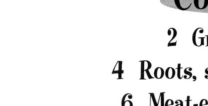

TWO CAN ™

Green world

Did you know that you share this planet with more than 375,000 different kinds of plants? Your green neighbours grow all over the place — in gardens and deserts and on snowy mountaintops.

Old timers

Plants have been around for more than 400 million years. That's before the dinosaurs roamed the Earth! The first kinds of plants were small and simple. In time, plants developed into giant, leafy tree ferns and thick, spongy mosses. Flowering plants first appeared about 135 million years ago.

Delicious! And so many kinds to choose from!

That's weird

Mushrooms and sea anemones may look like plants — but they're not! They belong to different groups of living things. Mushrooms are a kind of fungus and sea anemones are tiny wriggling animals!

BEWARE!
Plant imposters

Mushroom   Sea anemone

Take a deep breath

The next time you pass a plant, stop and thank it. Not only is it pretty to look at, but it also helps you stay alive. Plants give off an important gas, called oxygen. This is the same gas that you need to breathe! Plants take in carbon dioxide, the same gas that you breathe out.

Thanks a lot!

OXYGEN

▲ Ferns are most at home in damp, shady spots, so this rainforest in New Zealand is a perfect place for them to grow. There are more than 10,000 different types of ferns in the world.

Roots, stems and leaves

Plants look peaceful on the surface, but inside it's a different story. Spreading roots, sturdy stems and green leaves work as a team to keep the plant alive.

Cooking up a storm

Each leaf is like a chef in a kitchen. It makes food for the plant by mixing up water and carbon dioxide. Sunlight is the secret ingredient that turns this recipe into a nutritious meal.

Root adventure

Some roots dig deep in the ground like hardworking miners. The roots suck up fresh water and nourishing minerals that help the plant to grow.

On the road

The plant's stem is like a busy moterway. Water from the roots and food from the leaves are delivered to other parts of the plant.

HA HA! What do you call a young plant? Bud. HEE HEE!

4

Under the microscope

Did you know that leaves are covered with tiny breathing holes? Carbon dioxide travels into the holes. Oxygen and water travel out.

Stem power

A liana's stem is particularly impressive. In the hot rainforest the stem works like a vacuum cleaner, sucking water up the plant at a rate of one metre a minute. The stem is also really strong — a hefty orang-utan could use it as a swing!

Hey guys! Come on up!

▲ Some rainforest trees have giant roots that snake across the ground and anchor the trees firmly in the wet soil.

Meat-eating

Most plants make their own food. A few, including some plants that live in places with little sunlight or not enough minerals, have to catch extra snacks. These sinister meat-munchers set clever traps to catch all kinds of animals, from fleas and flies to frogs!

Aaagh!

Eeek!

Ribbit!.

▲ Watch out for this Venus's fly-trap – it's lethal! When a tasty treat hops into the plant's jaw-like leaves, they snap shut. The plant feeds on the animal's juices. Yummy!

mOnsters

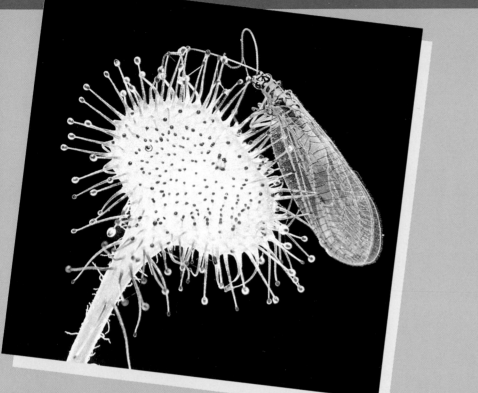

Sticky problem

If an insect lands on a sundew leaf, it quickly comes to a sticky end. The leaf is covered with hundreds of hairs, each with a gluey bead on the end. When the insect gets stuck on the beads, the leaf curls over and dinner is served!

Underwater terror

A bladderwort sucks its victims into a watery grave. The stems of this underwater plant have hollow pouches with secret trapdoors. When a creature, such as a mosquito larva, touches a trapdoor, the door opens. Water rushes into the pouch taking the larva with it. The larva is then devoured.

Help! Let me out!

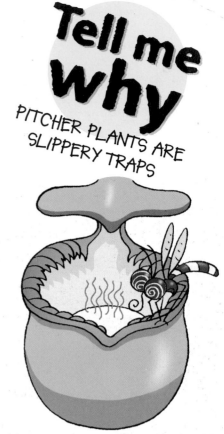

This sneaky rainforest plant has slippery leaves that catch its dinner. An insect lands on the rim of a pitcher-shaped leaf, enticed by the plant's sweet smell. Little does it know that it's heading into a deadly trap.

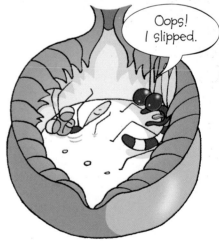

Oops! I slipped.

Before long, the victim loses its footing. It slips and slides down the wall of the leaf and lands in a murky pool of water at the bottom. The plant releases an acid and the insect turns to mush. Burp!

Fabulous flowers

POLLINATION—A SPECIAL DELIVERY

Flowers come in hundreds of shapes, sizes and colours — and they nearly all make seeds. Animals often help flowers with this tricky task by carrying tiny grains, called pollen, from flower to flower.

To make seeds, a flower needs to be dusted with pollen grains from another flower. This is called pollination. A hummingbird is perfect for making these pollen deliveries.

The hummingbird flies to a flower attracted by the plant's sweet nectar. As it drinks the nectar, the bird's head and beak get covered with hundreds of pollen grains.

Refreshed, the hummingbird takes off. When it flies to another flower for a sip, the hummingbird drops off its crucial pollen package and picks up another.

Bee my valentine

This sneaky orchid lures male bees looking for a mate — the centre part of the flower looks like a female bee! When the male lands on the flower, the pollen on the bee's body brushes off onto the flower.

That's weird

Carlos Linnaeus was a scientist with green fingers. In the 18th century, he grew his own personal flower clock. He planted a circle of flowers carefully chosen for his garden. Each one opened up at a different time of the day!

Ah! It's lunchtime.

Prepare to land

A monkey flower is like an airport runway. The flower's markings show bees where to land and find the plant's tasty nectar. These markings are visible only to bees!

▲ One of the world's largest flowers is the gigantic rafflesia. It grows up to one metre across and has no stem or leaves.

Sowing the seeds

Before most seeds can grow into new plants, they need a patch of soil and plenty of sunlight and water. Seeds may float on water or drift on the wind for miles in search of the right spot. A few even hitch rides to their new homes.

We have liftoff

A squirting cucumber plant gives its seeds a spectacular send-off. As a cucumber ripens, it fills up with water. The pressure builds until suddenly the cucumber explodes and blasts into the air just like a space rocket. The seeds shoot out and fall to the ground.

Under the microscope

The fruit of the avens plant is covered with tiny hooks. When a hairy animal brushes against these hooks, they catch onto the animal's fur. After a long, bumpy ride, the fruit's seeds fall off in a new home.

Flying squadrons

Dandelion seeds are perfectly equipped to travel on the wind — they float like parachutes. Each seed hangs from a tiny stem that has feathery hairs at the top. One gust of wind and the seeds can drift for miles.

Coconut palm seeds are long-distance ocean travellers. They can drift up to 1,930 kilometres before reaching dry land!

▲ Many coconut palm seeds make ocean voyages, each inside a huge waterproof shell that's packed with food and water. The seeds may travel for up to two years before sprouting on a faraway beach.

Tremendous trees!

From towering redwoods to bulging baobabs and waving palms, trees are magnificent. They are the biggest plants of all and live longer than anything else on Earth.

10 years

1 year

8 years

...?

Guess my age!

How old am I?

Did you know that many trees keep track of their age? They use rings to do it! Each ring equals one year of growth. These rings are different sizes — the thicker the ring, the more the tree grew that year. It would take a long time to count the rings of a really old tree!

▲ Redwoods are the world's tallest trees. They soar up to 111 metres, that's taller the Statue of Liberty, USA.

That's weird

A banyan tree just can't stop growing new trunks and roots. One tree in India has 1,700 pillar-like trunks supporting its branches. It's so wide that it could hide more than 1,000 schoolchildren.

Water, water!

You'll never be left dying of thirst next to a traveller's palm. The tree stores water at the bottom of each leafstalk. When a groove is cut into the leafstalk, a thirst-quenching drink gushes out.

Hey, stop! I've had enough now!

Terrific trunk

An African baobab tree is a peculiar sight. Its bulging trunk can grow up to 15 metres wide. But this strange-looking tree is incredibly useful. People eat the fruit and flowers. They also make medicines, rope, cloth and paper from the leaves, roots and tough bark.

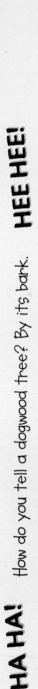

Under attack

Plants can't run away, so they're in constant danger from leaf-chewing animals. But plants do have a few tricks, such as sneaky disguises and sharp thorns. They may also get help from plant-friendly insects.

Ouch! Just one — ouch — more bite.

▲ This goat is having a hard time eating its lunch. The prickly thorns on the branches of this acacia tree protect it like a suit of armour and stop the goat from chomping on too many leaves.

ANT PROTECTION

My turn for guard duty.

A bull's horn acacia is protected by a fierce army of ants that lives inside the plant's large thorny stems.

When an animal tries to munch the leaves, the patrolling ants sound the alarm! They bite the intruder until it gives up.

Take that!

Could you pass the salt?

In return, the tree provides them with yummy take-out meals, which the ants tear from the leaf tips.

Stone me!

One kind of desert plant looks like pebbles! In stony parts of the Namib Desert, the leaves of pebble plants are shaped and patterned to look like stones. Hungry porcupines just step over the plants, unaware of the tasty snacks beneath their feet.

There must be something to eat around here.

That's weird

A strangler fig is one of the few plants that goes on the attack, but its victims are other plants! This deadly assassin wraps its stems around a rainforest tree and climbs towards the sunlight. When the strangler fig steals all the light and water, the tree dies.

Wow! That's some hug!

What's your poison?

A plant is not always as innocent as it looks! Pretty foxgloves, delicate rose bay shrubs and even plain old nettles are just a few plants whose leaves and stems are packed full of poison.

Beware

Plant poison can be really harmful. Eating just a few foxglove leaves makes a person's heart beat so fast that he or she could die in a few minutes! Never eat plants unless you're sure they're safe.

Toxic!

Take care

But foxglove leaves are lifesavers, too. They are used in tiny amounts by doctors to treat heart attacks. The foxglove poison stimulates a person's heart to start it beating again.

This should do the trick.

Under the microscope

Do you know why brushing against nettle plants is so painful? Nettles are covered with tiny needle-sharp hairs. When the hairs pierce your skin, they inject a poison that causes an itchy rash.

Poisonous partnership

The rose bay shrub provides one type of grasshopper with a handy weapon. This cunning grasshopper sucks poisonous sap out of the plant's leaves and stores it inside its body. When a bird attacks the grasshopper, the poison oozes out, leaving a nasty taste in the bird's mouth.

Master of disguise

A plant called the dead nettle doesn't make poison. Instead, it fools animal nibblers by looking like its painful stinging neighbour. The dead nettle is such a convincing mimic that any animal that's had a brush with a real nettle plant keeps its distance.

▲ A glory lily is one of the world's most poisonous plants. Every part of this African plant is poisonous, from the roots to the petals.

THE BORGIA FAMILY USED BELLADONNA

In the 1700s, in Italy, the wicked Borgia family became famous for poisoning people. They used a plant called deadly nightshade, or belladonna. The Borgias used the juice from the plant's berries to make a deadly potion.

Then they invited people who had annoyed them to dinner. This is when the Borgias secretly slipped the poisonous potion into the wine or food of their unlucky guests.

Desert dwellers

Desert plants have a tough life. They have to put up with scorching daytime temperatures and little or no rain for months or even years. But desert plants are hardy, finding plenty of crafty ways to stay alive.

Lost limb

When water is scarce, a quiver tree takes drastic measures. It lets the ends of its branches drop off so the precious water has fewer places to go!

I'm getting out of here!

Water thief

An Australian plant called a Christmas tree is a ruthless bandit. This tree steals water from neighbouring plants. Its roots slice through the roots of other plants and slurp up every last drop of water inside. The tree steals enough water to flower at Christmas, the hottest time of year in Australia.

Boing! Boing! Boing!

Restless drifter

A tumbleweed spreads its seeds far and wide. Every autumn, as this restless plant dries out, it turns into a hollow ball and eventually uproots itself. When the wind blows, the plant rolls along the plains leaving behind a trail of seeds that will grow into new wandering plants.

A saguaro cactus can store more than one tonne of water in its stem and arms — that's enough water to fill up 13 bathtubs. Its tough skin and sharp spines keep thirsty animals away.

Life in the freezer

Imagine battling against freezing-cold temperatures and howling winds. Plants that grow in the icy Arctic and on snowy mountains survive these challenges for months at a time!

Who are you calling a snowman?

▲ Fir trees survive long, cold winters even when they are cloaked in ice and snow. Their narrow leaves, called needles, have a waxy coating to keep moisture in and the cold out.

Success story

You don't look a day over 9,999.

In 1954, in Canada, a group of plant-loving explorers dug up a group of Arctic lupin seeds that had lain frozen in the soil for more than 10,000 years. Amazingly, when the seeds were replanted, some of them flowered.

Bang or bounce?

Cushion plants are low-growing plants that sprawl across cold mountain tops. They have thousands of shoots that are packed tightly together to keep in the warmth. The plants look spongy enough to bounce on, but they're really as hard as rock!

Ouch!

THUD!

I'm first!

FINISH

Early riser

Every spring, alpine snowbells race to flower and sow their seeds before the short summer is over. Beneath the melting snow, the fast-acting buds soak up the heat from the Sun's rays. In no time at all, they are blooming.

Tell me why

A FEW PLANTS WEAR FUR COATS

Brrr.

The tree groundsel is a giant plant that grows high on Mount Kenya in Africa. It keeps a snug layer of its dead leaves wrapped around its trunk. This leafy layer, which is like a fur coat, helps to keep the tree warm on chilly nights.

Nighty-night!

The saussurea plant makes its home high in the Himalayan mountains. Its full-length coat, which looks like wool, keeps the cold air away. The coat is so cosy that even insects snuggle up inside for the night!

Steamy rainforest

More types of plants grow in hot, damp rainforests than anywhere else in the world. Rainforests are jam-packed full of towering trees, creeping vines and giant flowers.

In the swim

Feel like taking a dip in your own private pool? Then track down a tank plant. These green wonders have watertight leaves to catch pools of rainwater. The pools are so inviting that frogs sometimes set up home there.

Climbing to the top

A liana climbs up trees towards the sunlight. It can reach 300 metres — that's higher than the Chrysler Building in New York, USA!

That's weird

Imagine hearing the sound of cannon fire in the Amazon rainforest! This noise happens when the hard fruits of the cannonball tree crash together in the wind.

POW!

Drip, drip!

It's easy to keep dry in the rainforest — just seek shelter under a leaf. Many rainforest leaves are large and have long, thin tips to help water roll off. They make great umbrellas!

Believe it or not
You'd have to be lucky to spot a titan arum flower. It blooms just once every seven years and lasts for only two days.

Now you see me — and now you don't!

▲ The flowering spike of a titan arum grows taller than a person. But don't inspect it too closely. This monster flower gives off a smell of rotting fish that will have you running for cover.

HA HA! What's worse than a scary flower? A creepy vine. **HEE HEE!**

23

▲ Amazon water lily plants have giant leaves that spread out over rivers and ponds, soaking up the light. Their gleaming white flowers can grow up to 30 centimetres across.

Water garden

Water lilies and water hyacinths have no problem finding a drink — they live in ponds and rivers! Water hyacinths float freely on the surface while water lilies have extra-long stems to anchor them firmly in place.

ON THE MARCH

> There were only a few plants here yesterday!

Water hyacinths spread like wildfire, creeping over the entire surface of a pond in just a few days. They cause serious problems.

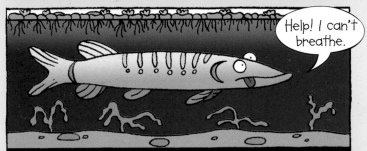

> Help! I can't breathe.

The fast-growing plants block out sunlight and use up the oxygen in the water. Fish and other plants in the pond choke and die.

POW!

People have tried everything to stop water hyacinths taking over, but even dynamite hasn't worked! These relentless water plants just keep coming back.

Land ahoy!

Did you know that an Amazon water lily is as strong as a boat? Rows of thick veins run along the bottom of each leaf. These veins are like the steel bars that support a bridge or a building. They keep the leaf so flat and strong that a small child can sit on it without fear of sinking!

25

Multipurpose plants

It's hard to imagine our lives without plants. We eat plants and use things made from them, such as wood, paper and fuel. Without our leafy helpers, we'd have no jeans to wear and no comics to read!

Believe it or not

Over a quarter of the world's medicines contain parts of plants. They are used to help treat everything from colds to cancer.

Reed and write

About 5,000 years ago, the ancient Egyptians made the world's first writing paper from papyrus reeds. They sliced the plants' stems into strips and crushed them together to make sheets of paper, called scrolls. They wrote on the paper with inks made from berries, barks and linseed oil.

This is harder than I thought!

▲ The milky sap from rubber trees is used to make tyres, rubber bands and tennis balls.

FROM COTTON TO JEANS

Did you know that your denim jeans are made from fluffy balls of fibre that grow around the seeds of cotton plants? Jeans were first made in the 1850s in the United States.

To make the first jeans, people picked cotton balls by hand from cotton plants. Then they spun these balls into long threads.

The threads were woven into cloth. When the fabric was stitched into trousers, jeans were invented. Jeans were popular during the California gold rush of the mid-1800s.

Jeans were made especially for the gold miners because the trousers were so sturdy. Still popular today, jeans come in many colours and all kinds of styles.

Fill it up!

Plants may be the fuel of the future. In Brazil, many cars run on ethanol, a fuel made from the sugarcane plant. And one day, people may be filling up their tanks with sap from the petrol plant as well.

That's weird

A few people claim that a forked hazel twig has helped them to find water hidden underground. They hold the twig in front of them as they walk. As soon as the twig twitches, they start digging!

Tall tales

There are plenty of myths and legends about the magical powers of plants. Many tall tales are based on a plant's real characteristics, such as its peculiar shape.

Climbing high

In the fairytale, Jack and the Beanstalk, a young boy grows a giant bean plant. The idea for this magical story probably came from the runner bean. This climbing plant is well known for how quickly it grows.

That's weird

In Haiti, it is claimed that drinking a potion made from thorn apple fruits will turn a person into a zombie. In tales, these walking dead are forced to become slaves.

Hey, watch out!

An unearthly cry

A mandrake root is shaped a bit like a human being. In medieval times, people believed this root was perfect for casting spooky spells. But there was one big problem — people also believed that the root cried out when it was pulled from the ground. If people heard the anguished scream, they were sure to die. Medieval sorcerers solved this problem by wearing earplugs!

Eeughaaah!

Huh, did you say something?

▲ Meat-eating plants provided the idea for this 1960s movie. In the movie, killer plants take over the Earth. They strangle their victims and then suck them dry.

Forget-me-not

The ancient Greeks believed that the fruit of the lotus plant made people lose their memories. A famous poem called the Odyssey, by the Greek poet Homer, told how sailors were washed up on a remote land and ate the lotus fruit. The magic food made the sailors forget their families and homeland completely.

Now, what was my name again?

Believe it or not

Some people believe that plants grow better to music! Research has shown that vibrations can make seeds sprout more quickly.

Plant show

Welcome to the greatest plant show on Earth! The star attractions include an ancient tree and a seed bigger than a football!

Hey, tree, give us a smile!

wollemi pine

Prize seed

Make sure you're not sitting underneath a coco de mer tree when its seeds are about to fall! This tree grows the largest and heaviest seeds in the world. A whopper can weigh as much as 20 kilograms. Long ago, people wondered where coco de mer seeds came from. They were always found floating in the sea. Then, in 1768, the mystery was solved — the coco de mer tree was discovered on the Seychelle Islands in the Pacific Ocean.

Double winner

The prize for the fastest growing plant goes to the bamboo. In just one day, this tall grass can shoot up one metre. That's incredible! Bamboo also wins the prize for the noisiest plant. As it grows, it squeaks and whines!

Be quiet, I'm trying to sleep!

Space traveller

Can you imagine rocketing into space? Well, a plant called Arabidopsis did in 1982. Russian scientists took this leafy traveller on board a space station to see if it could grow seeds in space. Mission accomplished — the plant grew seeds.

Ancient wonder

Bristlecone pines grow in the White Mountains in eastern California. Scientists have taken samples from the pines and discovered that some of them are over 4,700 years old — making them the oldest trees in the world. The gnarled trunks of these ancient plants are mostly dead, with only a few needles to show that they are still alive.

Index

Published by Two-Can Publishing, a division of Zenith Entertainment plc, 43-45 Dorset Street, London W1H 4AB. www.two-canpublishing.com

© Two-Can Publishing 2000
For information on Two-Can books and multimedia, call (0)20 7224 2440, fax (0)20 7224 7005, or visit our website at http://www.two-canpublishing.com

Created by act-two, 346 Old Street, London EC1V 9RB

Authors: Deborah Kespert and Julia Hillyard
Illustrations: Andrew Peters
Consultant: Dr. Sandra Knapp
Photographs: Cover: Heather Angel/Biofotos; p1: Bruce Coleman Ltd; p3: Tony Stone Images; p5: Oxford Scientific Films; p5 (top): Science Photo Library; p6: Oxford Scientific Films; p7: Bruce Coleman Ltd; p8: Planet Earth Pictures; p9: Bruce Coleman Ltd; p10: Planet Earth Pictures; p11: Oxford Scientific Films; p12: Tony Stone Images; p13: Planet Earth Pictures; p14: NHPA; p16: Science Photo Library; p17: The Garden Picture Library; p18: FLPA; p19: NHPA; p20: Oxford Scientific Films; p22: NHPA; p23: Heather Angel/Biofotos; pp24-25: Bruce Coleman Ltd; p26: Oxford Scientific Films; p28: ET Archive; p30: FLPA; p31: Bruce Coleman Ltd.

Every effort has been made to contact the copyright owner of the poster image reproduced on page 29.

Two-Can hopes to be able to correct this omission in future editions of the book.
'Two-Can' is a trademark of Two-Can Publishing.
Two-Can Publishing is a division of Zenith Entertainment plc,
43-45 Dorset Street, London W1H 4AB

ISBN: 1-85434-804-3
10 9 8 7 6 5 4 3 2 1

Dewey Decimal Classification 581

A catalogue record for this book is available from the British Library.

Printed in Singapore